BIGGEST EVENING SALE IN THE WORLD

Evening News

London Thursday October 25, 1973   No. 28,526   3p

'RUSSIANS FOR SUEZ' —U.S. ALERTS NUCLEAR FORCES

BOMBERS, TROOPS, MISSILES ON 'PRECAUTIONARY STAND-BY'

Scramble . . . A giant B-52 bomber of the U.S. Air Force.

WASHINGTON, Thursday

THE UNITED STATES today placed key units of its armed forces, including the nuclear strike force, on alert after receiving a warning from Moscow that Russia might send troops to the Middle East to enforce the ceasefire.

The "low level" alert, still well short of any war threat level, went to air force, army and navy units in the U.S., Europe and the Pacific. Washington government sources reported.

The Defence Department refused to confirm reports of the alert or to discuss the situation in any way.

The alert involved elements of the Strategic Air Command which includes America's nuclear strike forces and the 82nd Airborne Division at Fort Bragg, North Carolina, the elite paratroop force available for dispatch to anywhere in the world on short notice.

Among the air bases on alert were Malmstrom at Great Falls, Montana, the site of America's Minuteman intercontinental ballistic missiles.

The 'six-ring' secret

An officer at Malmstrom said a "six-ring alert" was in effect. He said the definition of "six-ring" was secret information.

Other bases included Plattsburg, New York, the home of B52 bombers. An official said the alert was flashed to the base in the middle of the night.

One senior Defence Department official asked if America was under threat of a nuclear attack replied firmly: "No."

The United States rejected yesterday an appeal by President Sadat that both the United States and Russia send troops to enforce the UN cease-fire, which Sadat claimed the Israelis were violating.

U.S. Government sources said the Soviet Union sent word to Washington that it was prepared to act alone if the United States did not join in an effort to stop violations of the cease-fire.

Russia was said to have banned Israel for any continued fishing in the Suez Canal area.

First reports of the alert of the U.S. forces and the prospect of two armies facing each other across the Suez Canal came as Mr Heath was speaking at a Cabinet meeting.

Among other things, it was already reviewing the Middle East crisis.

The British Government had been given no advance warning and there was a flurry of diplomatic activity in Whitehall.

Britain's first response will be to step up efforts to get a properly constituted UN force on the scene as fast as possible.

It is stated authoritatively in Whitehall that British troops are ready and available to join the UN force if required.

BIG TWO FACE CRUNCH

By JOHN DICKINSON
Evening News Political Editor

THE hair - raising prospect of a super - power confrontation set alarm bells ringing furiously in London this afternoon.

Sharp worry

Government sources said U.S. concern was heightened by intelligence information that a significant number of Soviet AN transport planes and ships were seen on route to the Middle East.

The sources said that intelligence experts suggested that the planes were not carrying troops.

The Russians have cut down their supply airlift to Egypt and Syria in recent days and the increase in flights had raised sharp worry.

Soviet Envoy's car spotted

There were reports that the National Security Council, the top foreign and military policy body under President Nixon, met during the night.

Secretary of State Henry Kissinger remained in his office through the night and Soviet Ambassador Anatoly Dobrynin's car was seen in the State Department's basement beneath Kissinger's office.

And it was confirmed this afternoon that Kissinger did meet the Russian envoy. Mr Kissinger was to give a Press conference late this evening.

Liner explosion

Le Havre, Thursday.—One man was killed and two injured in an explosion in the engine-room of the liner France in Le Havre today.

Police storm jail

Melun, France, Thursday.—Riot police, helped by firemen with ladders, stormed Melun jail, to quell a protest by 100 prisoners.

Six Asians seized in dawn raid on West End

Evening News Reporter

SIX ASIANS believed to be illegal immigrants were seized today by the police in a dawn raid in the West End.

They were being held at Marylebone Lane police station.

Asians living at a six-storey house at Victoria Mansions, Hanson Street, near the Post Office Tower, were awakened by police checking passports.

SLEEPLESS

More than a dozen police with cars sealed off Hanson Street as officers entered the house.

An elderly white woman who lives near stated after the raid that she had watched Asians unloaded from covered lorries during the night on several occasions.

She said: "I have five or six Indians carrying small cases rush out of lorries, into Victoria Mansions.

"The drivers were always white."

A Scotland Yard spokesman said: "Six coloured men were taken to Marylebone Lane police station where they are being interviewed by Home Office immigration officials."

It was mid-day and he had

A Minuteman missile speeds to its target.

SHARES PLUNGE AS POUND SLIPS

Millions of pounds were wiped off share prices on the Stock Market following the U.S. forces alert.

Oils like BP and Burmah plunged by as much as 10p at one stage. Government stocks fell by up to 50p and leading industrials like ICI, Reckitt and Colman, Courtaulds and Pilkingtons by 2p to 3p.

The pound tumbled to points to 2·4395 against the dollar, but quickly picked up again to 2·4410.

MOTHER OF PEARL

Mr Mum is very good at knitting.—Croydon girl.

Dayan offer to quit but Golda says no

TEL AVIV, Thursday

ISRAEL'S Defence Minister Moshe Dayan offered to quit today over criticism of the country's preparedness for the latest Middle East war.

Mr Dayan made a statement replying to the demand of Justice Minister Yaakov Shapiro that he should resign.

The newspaper Haaretz and Mr Shapira was critical of the country's state of readiness for the October Egyptian and Syrian attack.

But Prime Minister Golda Meir said Dayan had complete confidence of Minister of Defence.

"Questions about the conduct of or of the war will be discussed in the after the war, as in time," she said.

And Mrs Meir reveals

Dayan had already offered his resignation to her a few days ago. She had refused it.

The Defence Minister's statement said he was responsible to the Cabinet and Knesset (parliament) not to the personal demands or complaints of an individual minister.

Military sources have said that a pre-emptive strike by Israel was compelled before

---

Keith Richard pictured with Anita Pallenberg

My life with drugs, by Stones star

By JOHN BLAKE

ROLLING STONE Keith Richard, fined £205 for possessing drugs and firearms, has talked for the first time about the dangers and temptations of drugs in the world of pop stars.

He is not a drug addict, he told me, although he has often been deeply involved with drugs.

Now, he says, he plans to avoid further clashes with the law.

I talked to the 29-year-old guitarist in his Mayfair hotel while he was waiting for the drug case to be heard at Marlborough Street court.

It was mid-day and he had just woken up. He wore tasty jeans and a T shirt and wandered bare foot about the lush suite.

With him was his girl friend Anita Pallenberg, 31, who yesterday was given a year's conditional discharge for possessing the drug Mandrax. Also in the hotel room were their two children Marlon, four, and Dandy, aged one.

"When I first started playing with the Stones I had never seen a joint, a sleeping pill or any kind of dope," he said.

"I didn't even know what they looked like and people used to come up to me and say 'What are you on, man?'

"Everybody assumed we were stoned out of our minds all the time. But I used to drink rum, and that was the heaviest thing I was on."

He went on: "I had very, very little to do with drugs. But since, I have been around a lot of people who were into drugs.

"I mean the disc jockeys in America get an ounce of cocaine to play a record. It is amazing in the States. Dope is everywhere."

I've tried everything

He then said: "Without being too explicit, I have tried everything."

But he added: "Dope plays a very small part in my life. I am really non interested in it. I have always been able to be naturally high.

"And after all I have been a father for four years and you can't really be stoned out of your mind when you've got kids running around.

"I mean, before the kids arrived I tried LSD, heroin and cocaine. But, I've never been strung out on any of those."

Keith Richard then told me that pop stars are sent drugs through the post, especially when they are on American tours.

"The stuff we get sent is unbelievable."

Very tired

He went on: "Then you find little packets of white powder in your dressing room. You can't get away from it.

"When you come back to this country the English customs start looking through your luggage and find three sleeping pills or something and then want to know every detail about how you got them.

"I mean, how can you get through to them what it's like to be tired?"

WHEN I WAS YOUNG

THE SEVENTIES

NEIL THOMSON
MEETS
TARUN PATEL

FRANKLIN WATTS

LONDON • NEW YORK • SYDNEY • TORONTO

Tarun Patel was born in Uganda in East Africa in 1965.
He is now a British citizen and lives in London. Tarun's
grandparents came from Gujerat in India and settled in
Uganda when both countries were under British rule.

Uganda gained independence in 1962, and nine years
later the government of Milton Obote was overthrown by
Idi Amin. In 1972 Amin ordered all the Asians living in
Uganda to leave. More than fifty thousand people were
forced to abandon their homes and businesses. Many
came to Britain to make a new life.

Tarun left Uganda with his mother when he was six and
came to London. He has lived since then in north-west
London where he went to school and college. Tarun is an
economics graduate and now works as a financial
consultant with a firm in Harrow.

Copyright © 1990 Franklin Watts Limited

First published in Great Britain by
Franklin Watts Limited
96 Leonard Street
London EC2A 4RH

Franklin Watts Australia
14 Mars Road
Lane Cove
N.S.W. 2066

ISBN: 0 7496 0238 4

CONTENTS

Born in Uganda

My name is Tarun Patel. I was born in Kampala in Uganda in 1965. My dad was called Chandrakant Patel. He worked as a motor engineer and his job took him all over East Africa. He died in a road accident when I was very young. I never had any brothers or sisters.

I lived with my mother and my grandmother in a house in Coronation Street in Kampala. My mum was born in Kampala, where her dad had a grocery business. He'd come originally from Gujerat in India, where we still have relatives in his village.

My mum, dad and I when I was very young.

My parents' marriage was arranged by my grandparents.

My dad was born in Kenya and went to Scotland to study engineering.

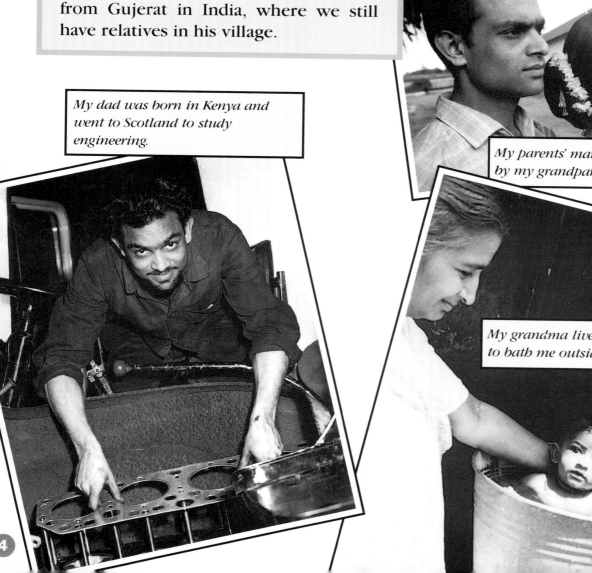

My grandma lived with us; she used to bath me outside.

4

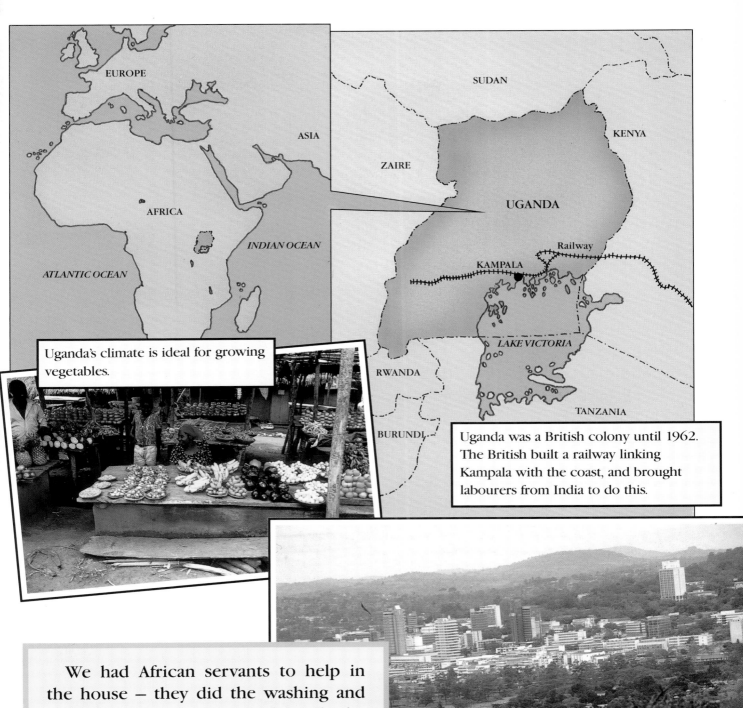

EUROPE

ASIA

AFRICA

ATLANTIC OCEAN

INDIAN OCEAN

SUDAN

ZAIRE

KENYA

UGANDA

Railway

KAMPALA

LAKE VICTORIA

RWANDA

BURUNDI

TANZANIA

Uganda's climate is ideal for growing vegetables.

Uganda was a British colony until 1962. The British built a railway linking Kampala with the coast, and brought labourers from India to do this.

We had African servants to help in the house – they did the washing and cleaning but my mum did all the cooking. We spoke Swahili with the servants and Gujerati, our own language, with family and friends. We had a two-hour siesta every afternoon when it was hot. There was plenty of good food and everything was very easy.

Kampala is an expanding modern city.

Exodus

In Uganda most of the shops and businesses were run by Asians like us. We weren't rich but we had a comfortable life. It all changed when Idi Amin came to power and said that all the Asians would have to leave. We were given seventy-two hours to get out. Everybody was in a panic about where they were going to go.

My dad had lived in Britain and we had British passports, so my mum decided to take me and my grandma to London. As soon as we could, we got tickets and went to Entebbe airport. There were army checkpoints everywhere and the soldiers made sure you weren't taking any valuables out. The army kept a bonfire burning and people were made to throw their suitcases on it. We just gave the servants the keys to the house and the car and left, taking only the clothes we were wearing and a few pounds. We were poor when we arrived in London.

Idi Amin was an army officer who seized power in 1971.

Asian shops were closed and abandoned by their owners.

Baggage had to be left behind at Entebbe airport.

WEATHER:
Dry, sunny.
Lighting-up time:
8.19 p.m.
Details—Back Page.   46,078

Evening Standard

London: Thursday August 31 1972   6   3p

From Mary Kenny, the only reporter to observe the airport tragedies of Uganda's departing Asians

STRIPPING OF THE BANISHED

Inflation warning: Barber plays it cool

By ROBERT CARVEL

CHANCELLOR Anthony Barber and his Treasury advisers stuck today to an optimistic view about Britain's economic prospects.

They did so in face of the forecast by the unofficial National Institute of Economic and Social Research that there will soon be a sharp acceleration in the rate of inflation, calling for strong measures to counter it.

It was acknowledged in Whitehall, however, that a great deal must depend on the outcome of the tripartite discussions now going on between the Government, the Confederation of British Industry and the Trades Union Congress.

These are aimed at restraining both prices and wages, and considerable importance is attached to the next meeting of the three sides arranged for September 14.

Unspoken thought

Nothing is officially admitted about possible changes in the direction of Government policy.

But the unspoken thought in official circles is that if this attempt by the Government to stabilise the position is unsuccessful then some more formalised kind of prices and incomes control will probably have to be devised within a few months.

As for the National Institute's prediction generally the Treasury view—based on its own bitter experiences—is that all economic forecasting is hazardous and who is to say that anybody is bound to be right?

● Inflation, the killer drug of Britain, by David Malbert.
—Page 35

Pound and shares hit Page 34

KAMPALA, Thursday.

I STOOD at Entebbe Airport, some 22 miles from Kampala, late last night and watched Asians check in for a flight departing to London. They were a despondent, melancholy collection of people.

A man stood at the Customs barrier with a watch and 60 Ugandan shillings in his hand, shaking his head glumly. "My friend was found with an extra watch and 60 shillings. He was told to leave them here." The friend departed for London divested of any extra possessions."

I went into the Customs Hall and saw a Customs officer slowly going through every item of baggage belonging to a young Asian couple, while their two small children cried and whimpered with a child's fatigue.

The Customs officer asked me my business. I said I wanted to find out if it was true that Asians were being stripped of their property at the airport.

'Madam.. it is our duty..'

"Well madam," he replied perfectly politely, "there are regulations which it is our duty to enforce. Come this way and I will show you."

He led me into a small office and pointed to a typed notice, marked with the stamp of the Collector of Customs and Excise, on the wall. This was a list of items which each departing Asian may take, namely.

● Two hundred kgs. of unaccompanied soft furnishings, such as bed sheets and blankets; all kitchenware prohibited, 20 kgs. of soft personal belongings.

● Fifty pounds per head of family foreign currency only, not one shilling of Ugandan money.

● In jewellery: one ring, one watch, two bangles, one necklace, one pair of ear-rings. Nothing to be more than 15 carat gold.

I asked the officer if everything over and above must be confiscated. "Yes," he replied. "These are the regulations; in some places we may use our discretion." He was a very reasonable man. "I am sorry about it, and I am sorry for them, but these are the regulations and we must enforce them."

The people were searched personally and he emphasised that there were two policewomen on duty to search women. I was then obliged to leave the Customs Hall, since I was not an outgoing passenger, and the customs man returned to searching the baggage of the Asian couple.

By chance, the army was not at the airport last night so things were relatively relaxed. I understand that everything is much tougher when there is a military presence; since all

Continued on Page 7

Hemery dazzles in Olympics

● More Olympic news and results .... Back Page

News on Camera and Olympic TV Guide .... Page 39

Rolls-Royce fiasco 'could happen again'
Page 10

British tourists may be stranded now
Page 5

Stock up the deep freeze now
Food News — Page 21

TV, radio .... Page 38

Letters .... Page 20

Entertainment - 16

Some Asian families went to Canada, others to Kenya, and some to India.

JOAN BAKEWELL, TV interviewer and former star of BBC-2's Late Night Line-up, has filed a divorce petition against her husband Michael Bakewell.

It appears in the undefended list to be heard in London. Joan, 38, names a woman called Morris.

The Bakewells met at Cambridge, where Joan was reading economics. They married in 1954. There are two children, aged 12 and eight.

Michael was head of BBC plays from 1964 to 1966.

Joan left Late Night Line Up at the end of July. She is now doing a Man Alive series called Times Remembered.

She is also doing 12 interviews for the religious department of the BBC under the title The Open Persuaders.

A new life in England

When we first arrived in England we went straight to my uncle's house in Harrow. He worked shifts at the Kodak factory. I was the youngest in the house. With my aunts, uncles and us there were nine people altogether in a three-bedroomed house.

Our first winter here I felt very cold, I always had to have an extra jumper on. It was the first time I'd ever seen snow. My uncle woke me up to see it at about two o'clock in the morning. It was a complete surprise.

We had to move when my uncle bought a newsagent's shop in Hoddesdon and the house was sold. It was difficult to find anywhere to live then as lots of people wouldn't let rooms to Asians. Mum found a house in Wembley and sublet some of the rooms to another Gujerati family to help pay the rent.

My second winter in England.

In the early 1970s there were few cars in Tarun's street.

The same street today.

We couldn't speak English when we first arrived in London. To begin with, we watched a lot of TV. We liked 'Magic Roundabout'; we learnt quite a bit of English from that. My grandma never learnt English so we always spoke Gujerati with her. She lives in India now.

An Asian friend helped Mum get a job at the local Post Office; it was the first job she'd had in her life. She worked there for fourteen years.

Wembley Observer

PUBLISHED TUESDAY AND FRIDAY

Friday, September 1, 1972

Price 4p

'Asian community in Wembley has proved exemplary in conduct'

NO COUNCIL HOUSES FOR THE REFUGEES

AS the first group of Asian refugees from Uganda prepares to come to Wembley, a statement has come from Brent Council that no local family will be put back on the housing waiting list because of the new arrivals.

Local leaders of the established Asian community in Wembley have promised to do all they can to see that no undue strain is placed on the borough's welfare services when the immigrants arrive.

The leader of Brent Council, Ald. P. H. Hartley, said this week that the practical problems of receiving the immigrants were not the greatest of the difficulties faced by Brent Council.

"How are we going to deal with the anxieties of our own people who fear the solution to their own social problems will be delayed because of the need to provide for the newcomers?" asked Ald. Hartley.

Stating that he did not think the numbers of immigrants coming to Wembley would be as high as had at first been predicted. Ald. Hartley made it clear that these families would not be given council houses.

'Will move on'

"There will be no prejudice to the chances of Brent residents already on the housing waiting list or approved for re-housing," he promised. "We shall not consider that any of these newcomers have the residential qualifications for municipal housing.

"Past experience has shown that Asian immigrants from Africa rarely ask for council housing. Those who come to Wembley will be doing so because

they have friends or relatives ready to put them up.

"In most cases, as soon as they will have found their feet, they will move on to settle where there is more accommodation. Those who stay in Brent will probably make their own arrangements for housing. As a community the Asians help each other and do not call on the council for help," he said.

Stating that he welcomed the Government's moves to try to keep Asian immigrants away from Brent and other crowded areas, Ald. Hartley made it clear that this was not because he had any complaints against the Asian community.

"The Asian community in Wembley has proved exemplarily in their conduct," he said.

ALTHOUGH newspaper reports from Uganda suggest that many of the Asians being expelled by President [...] in are considering coming to Wembley, Brent still [...] ks official information.

[...] here has been no new information available from the [...] ion Office on the distribution [...] the Asians, said a Brent [...] ncil spokesman, and no definite [...] n has been made on Brent's [...] cation for Government assistance with its schools problem. The request is still with the [...] Office, he added.

[...] ent's Director of Education Miss Gwen Rickras, had [...] with the Home Office late [...] eek. These were described [...] an exploration of the situation.

[...] s week the leader of the [...] ervatives on Brent Council, C. R. Sheppard, said that [...] ncil should press the [...] nment for exact information [...] n how many Ugandan [...] plan to settle in Wembley.

Mr. Sheppard said it should [...] en made quite clear to [...] vernment that Brent [...] accurate information [...] it could plan for the ex- [...] nflux.

Government should be [...] et the necessary infor- [...] from the Asians in [...] he said, and Brent [...] ave demanded the fi-

these people will stay, and large numbers come to Wembley, then we just won't have the power to do anything.

Ald. Hartley, the council leader, is not dealing with the problem with any method. He is just sitting on his backside and saying: 'Well, let them come. There won't be as many as everyone thinks and we can make arrangements when they come.'

"His attitude is like holding a big dinner, but not knowing how many people are going to come. How on earth can you be expected to cater for them?"

Nobody there to be rescued

Firemen wearing breathing apparatus entered a burning house in Swinderby Road, Wembley, on Sunday afternoon to check whether anyone was trapped.

The tenants of both the ground floor flat and the first floor flat were out when the fire broke out in a bedroom.

A passer-by raised the alarm and four pumps fought the fire.

The bedroom of the first floor flat was extensively damaged as well as part of the roof.

DETERMINED TO MAINTAIN STANDARDS

'Obviously these people have to go somewhere'

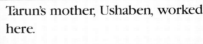

Tarun's mother, Ushaben, worked here.

Starting school

My mum went along to the nearest school to see if I could start there. The head said, "Your son will be the first Indian child in the school. I'll look after him". Mum started crying when the teacher was nice to her. She hardly spoke any English then although she could understand quite a bit. I couldn't speak English either so I wasn't any help at all.

It was all a bit of a shock to me, the whole thing was completely new. I couldn't understand the teacher, and the other kids in the class all had different coloured skin from me. It felt very strange. I'd been too young to go to school in Uganda so Mum felt lonely to begin with and sat outside the classroom all morning waiting for me to come out.

Tarun's primary school in the 1970s.

LONDON BOROUGH OF BRENT

LYON PARK PRIMARY SCHOOL

Desks from Tarun's old classroom.

Me on my friend's bike. I hadn't learnt how to ride it then.

I was pretty quiet at first, especially in breaktime, but then I started playing football and got quite excited. We had a light plastic ball so we couldn't break the windows. The girls and boys were kept separated in the playground by a line of teachers.

After school I'd go to my friend's house; we were the only two Asian boys in the class in my first year. His mum used to look after us until mine came to pick me up after she'd finished work. On Saturday there was no school, so no babysitting. I'd have to go to the Post Office with my mum. She worked and I sat by the counter. If I sat quietly until one o'clock, when she finished, we'd go to the newsagent and I'd get a chocolate.

Tarun's primary school today.

I'd buy a Curly Wurly or a Milky Way.

Playtime

I joined the Cubs early on. I belonged to the third Wembley troop. We met on Mondays and I always rushed home afterwards to watch "The Waltons" on telly. I couldn't wait for Arkala to say "Cubs, dismiss!" so that I could get back in time.

We had a craze for marbles; they came pretty high up the list for pocket money. I bought mine from the corner shop. It's run by Asians now but it wasn't then. I had over a thousand marbles; during break it was big business swapping and winning them.

When the conker season came, the marbles got packed away. There were special shaped conkers called the cheese and the double cheese, that was one with two flat edges. I got Mum to put them in the oven or the freezer to make them hard.

I always got pocket money from both my mum and my grandma, who lived with us. I did pretty well – better than most of my friends, I think. I had to account for every penny.

I saved a little in my Post Office piggy bank – Mum kept the key.

The Cubs met near our house.

3RD WEMBLEY SCOUT GROUP
SCOUTS FRI. 7·30
CUBS MON. 6·30

WEMBLEY & SUDBURY DISTRICT SCOUT COUNCIL

The Scout Association

Certificate

to

TARAN PATEL of the 3RD WEMBLEY Pack

on gaining Maximum Points (15) PLAIN BURCOTT Class

1975 Cub Scout Handicraft Competition.

22.11.1975.

District Commissioner.

Cub Scout
Handicraft Competition
22nd November 1975
Wembley & Sudbury Packs

Once I read English well I became really keen on comics, I had a big collection. I'd run down to the newsagent's with my pocket money after school and read the comics right there. I couldn't wait till I got home. Some of my friends collected stamps but I never did. That was funny, really, since it might have been easy with my mum working in the Post Office.

At school we collected football stickers, the favourites were Tottenham Hotspur. There was a newsagent's nearby which sold stickers but they only let two kids in at a time so we used to boycott it. That shop's gone now, it's a tandoori chicken place.

We went shopping for clothes to M&S on Wembley High Road. If we wanted special foods we had to go to Popat Stores on Ealing Road. That was the only Asian food store around then, now almost the whole road is Asian.

Today there are many successful Asian businesses in Wembley.

Ealing Road in the 1970s.

13

Secondary school

A few more Asian kids came to my primary school in my second year. Some of our neighbours were Asian and by my fourth year at that school there were quite a lot. When I went to secondary school, it was completely mixed.

We were given a New Testament at school, whatever our religion. Every morning we had a Christian assembly. You didn't have to sing the hymns if you were Asian, but I enjoyed it. Everybody said the prayers and you had to say them properly even if you didn't understand the words.

No one ever took the mickey out of me for being Asian. I was lucky, though, lots of Asian kids did suffer. Later on I was quite good at sports, and I think that helped me get accepted.

BRENT SCHOOLS' CRICKET ASSOCIATION

Awarded to Tarun Patel
of Park Lane Sc...
Runners up in North Brent 'A' League
July 1976

The main buildings of Alperton High School.

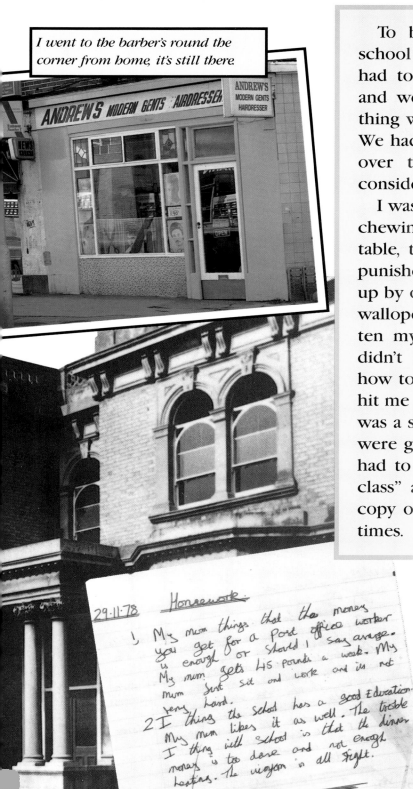

I went to the barber's round the corner from home, it's still there.

To begin with, my comprehensive school had a very strict uniform. We had to have our top button done up and we couldn't wear trainers. Everything we couldn't do we wanted to do. We had to have neat hair, it was all right over the ears but collar-length was considered long.

I was caned at school once. It was for chewing gum and sticking it under the table, there were three of us who got punished for that. I was never beaten up by other kids at school but I did get walloped by the PE teacher. I'd forgotten my kit two or three times and I didn't have an excuse. I didn't know how to make up good lies. The teacher hit me on the backside with a slipper, it was a size twelve and it really hurt. We were given lines for bad behaviour. We had to write out "I must not chew in class" and things like that. We had to copy out the line one or two hundred times.

My exercise book.

I wasn't in any of the gangs at school. There were always the tough guys and inter-school fights, but I didn't get involved. When I was fourteen the skinhead craze started. The skinheads had really short haircuts and often had tattoos. They wore Doc Marten boots, but they had to keep their trousers over the tops of their boots in school. They wrote "Skins" in all the books and called all the Asian kids "Paki". The skinheads all left the school before the sixth form so they didn't bother us for long.

Then there were the Teddy boys with Elvis haircuts and sharp-toed shoes, they never sat near the skinheads. When the teachers had to find kids to be prefects there wasn't much choice, once they'd excluded the Skins and the Teds, so I got to be a prefect.

Me in my school sweater, aged fourteen.

Groups like Showaddywaddy made Teddy boy styles fashionable.

Harold Wilson resigned as Prime Minister in 1976.

Margaret Thatcher was the first woman Prime Minister in Britain.

The chip shop near Tarun's school.

There weren't many punks at my school.

At school the teachers talked a bit about what was happening in the news. When Harold Wilson was Prime Minister some of us used to imitate him. We said, "The man with the pipe is our leader". During the General Election in 1979 we were asked what we would do if we were Prime Minister. I said, "Take all the money from the rich and give it to the poor".

I went down to the polling booth with my mum when she went to vote. I stayed up till three in the morning to see the results on TV. Then we got up early to watch the news with Thatcher getting in.

There were quite a few strikes while I was at school but we never had any days off. When the dinner ladies went on strike we all went out for lunch, and the chip shop down the road made a lot of money. We went to the park, ate chips, and made fun of the girls.

Entertainment

I liked most pop music and I loved "Top of the Pops". I watched it every week. My favourites were Gary Glitter and the Bay City Rollers. I had posters of them up in my room. I liked the Boomtown Rats too, they had a good beat. My schoolfriends went to pop concerts but I never did. I'd have liked to go but my mum didn't want me to, she'd have worried about it. I always had to tell her where I was going and what time I'd be back. I didn't much like Indian music then but I used to play the tabla. I've still got my old set. I liked playing that, it was all rhythm.

My friend played acoustic guitar. He was Spanish, and he was pretty good. Whatever he did I always wanted to do but I never learnt to play much, apart from the tune from the film "The Good, the Bad and the Ugly". We loved westerns.

"IN I ASKED READERS POP POLL" ELECTION.

The response was tremendous and below you will see the result.

Included in the list are the pop stars who received the most votes, and it should be remembered that the pop scene is ever changing and the most popular stars of last May are not necessarily the most popular today.

Take David Essex for example. When we ran the poll he was in America and had been out of the limelight while making a film. It could be that if I ran the poll today, he would be amongst the leaders.

...the result, and a big thank you to ...o took the trouble to write in.

4. ...dust
5. Osmonds (including Donny, Jimmy and Marie)
6. Suzi Quatro
6. Mud
7. Sweet
8. David Bowie
9. David Cassidy
10. Olivia Newton John
11. Bay City Rollers
12. Wizzard
Barry Blue

Capital Radio started broadcasting in 1973.

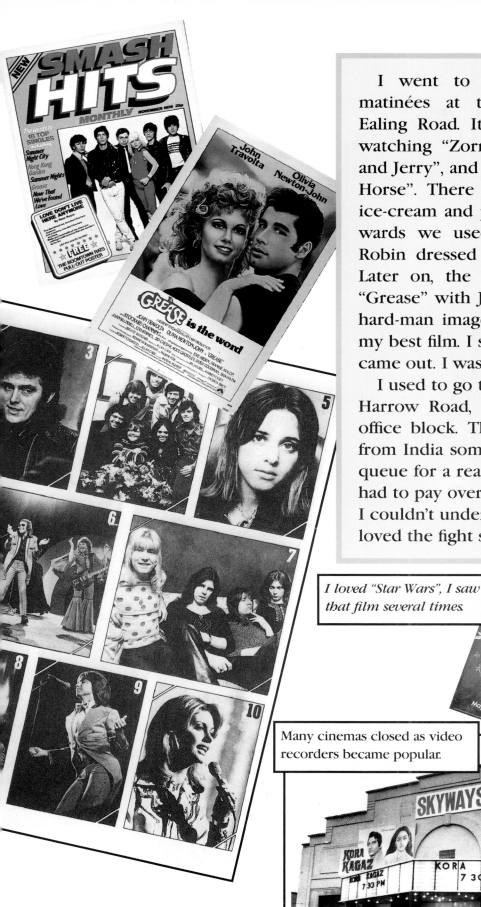

I went to the Saturday morning matinées at the Odeon cinema in Ealing Road. It was packed with kids watching "Zorro", cartoons like "Tom and Jerry", and "Champion, the Wonder Horse". There was always a break for ice-cream and popcorn. At home afterwards we used to play Batman and Robin dressed up in my mum's cape. Later on, the film I really liked was "Grease" with John Travolta, I liked his hard-man image and the music. It was my best film. I saw it twice when it first came out. I was thirteen then.

I used to go to the Liberty cinema on Harrow Road, that's gone now, it's an office block. They showed Hindi films from India sometimes. There'd be a big queue for a really popular film, and you had to pay over the odds to get a ticket. I couldn't understand the dialogue but I loved the fight scenes and the songs.

I loved "Star Wars", I saw that film several times.

Many cinemas closed as video recorders became popular.

Sports

When I was eleven we moved house to quite near Wembley Stadium. It was really good fun on Cup Final days. A couple of my friends would come round and we'd stand at the front of the house and watch the coaches going by. We waved at the fans of the team we supported and shouted "Boo" at the others. We got away with that because we were too small then for any trouble.

I collected cricketers' autographs. I managed to get nearly all the great ones. I used to hang around outside the ground after a match and wait for them to come out. I was a keen player until I broke my thumb and my collar bone while I was batting in the nets against a demon bowler.

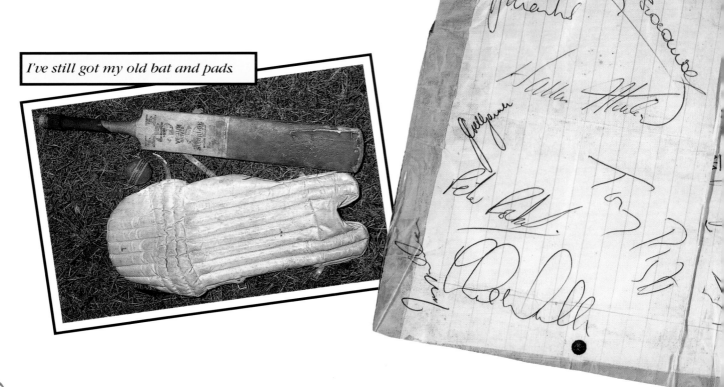

EMPIRE STADIUM WEMBLEY
Assoc. Football ENGLAND v ITALY 16/11/77

THE EMPIRE STADIUM, WEMBLEY

Association Football
INTERNATIONAL MATCH
(World Cup Qualifying)

ENGLAND
VERSUS
ITALY

No ticket genuine unless it carries a Lion's Head watermark below

WED. NOV. 16, 1977

KICK-OFF 7.45 p.m.
YOU ARE ADVISED TO TAKE UP YOUR POSITION BY 7.15 p.m.

J.S. Leith CHAIRMAN: WEMBLEY STADIUM LTD

STANDING
£2.50

TO BE RETAINED

TURNSTILES
C
ENTRANCE

10
EAST
UPPER
STANDING
ENCLOSURE

342

SEE PLAN AND CONDITIONS ON BACK

I went to the match at Wembley, England won.

I've still got my old bat and pads.

ENGLAND
Possible contenders

IAN BOTHAM. Somerset. 23. Right-arm medium bowler and right-hand bat. 23 wickets, and 291 runs in winter Tests.

GEOFF BOYCOTT. Yorkshire. 38. Right-hand opening batsman. Played in 80 Tests and has scored over a hundred centuries.

MIKE BREARLEY. Middlesex. 36. Right-hand batsman. Has led England in 19 tests, winning drawing 5 and losing one.

PHIL EDMONDS. Middlesex. 28. Left-arm spinner and right-hand batsman. Made Test debut v Australia in 1975.

JOHN EMBUREY. Middlesex. 26. Off-spin bowler. Took 16 wickets, av. 19.13 v Australia in winter.

MIKE GATTING. Middlesex. 21. Right-hand batsman, right-arm medium pace bowler and excellent fielder.

GRAHAM GOOCH. Essex. 25. All-rounder who scored 246 runs, av. 22.36 in last winter's series, with a top score of 74.

DAVID GOWER. Leicestershire. 22. Left-hand bat. Topped Test averages in Australia, scoring 420 runs, av. 42.

MIKE HENDRICK. Derbyshire. 30. Right-arm fast-medium bowler. Topped winter tour averages with 28 wickets, av. 14.25.

JOHN LEVER. arm fast right-hand wickets in

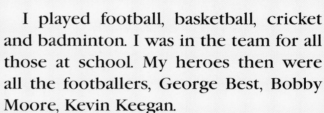

...medium and first-rate slip ...ed in 41 Tests.

...shire. ...bat. ...batting.

I supported the Campaign for Nuclear Disarmament.

I played football, basketball, cricket and badminton. I was in the team for all those at school. My heroes then were all the footballers, George Best, Bobby Moore, Kevin Keegan.

I played darts with my friends and a lot of ping-pong. I had my own bat and used to play down at the community centre.

I had to have a skateboard when the craze first started. It cost £10, that was a lot of money then. I had the pads and the whole kit and used to practise on the street.

I always dreaded going to swimming classes. In Uganda there weren't any pools and it was far from the sea so I'd never learnt to swim there. I did get my 10-metre certificate but then I gave it up. I hated cross-country running, I used to take a short cut and then wait for a few people to come by. Then I'd run the last bit and look whacked so the teachers wouldn't know I'd cheated.

Things to buy

My first birthday in England. I always got a big present.

We never had much money when I was young. Mum didn't earn much at her Post Office job and prices kept going up all the time. We never celebrated Christmas much at home, but Mum always asked me what I wanted for my birthday. One year digital watches had just come out and that was what I badly wanted, even though I already had an ordinary watch. I got one of those Texas Instruments ones with a little light.

My uncle used to buy me the more expensive presents – he got me a bike for my tenth birthday. It was a "Chopper", that was the in-thing then. I had a Casio calculator, it was thick and the buttons made a noise when you pressed them. We weren't allowed calculators in class till I was fifteen. We had to use slide rules and really had to know our times tables.

I had a Sony Walkman pretty soon after they came out. I never had a ghetto blaster, though lots of other kids did.

I learnt to use a slide rule to do calculations.

If your bike had three gears you were doing really well.

THE HOT ONE

Ride the bike with burn-up potential. Straddle the hottest number Raleigh have ever produced.

Chopper. A machine inspired by the screaming rubber and roaring fantails of the dragster racing slick.

Chopper, designed on lean, taut, tear-away-and-love-it lines. For guys and gals who want a bike built for action. With the lid off!

You've never known anything like Chopper. It took the U.S.A. by storm. With its high-rise "apehanger" handlebars. Coil-spring shock absorbers. Drag-style saddle. Chrome roll bar. And snap-action shift that flashes change of pace instantly from the crossbar.

Wow your pals on Chopper. Turn heads as you rip away. Own a machine with muscle to spare.

Chopper. The hot one!

CHOPPER

LCD

CASIO fx-29
SCIENTIFIC CALCULATOR

You're never too old

We didn't have a car. My mum never learnt to drive and, anyway, I don't think we could have afforded one

23

Weekends

On Sundays we always went to our temple in Islington. The temple is a very special place for us. We're members of a Hindu sect, followers of the Swami Narayan movement. When I was older the temple moved to a converted warehouse near where we lived. By that time the Saturday matinées had stopped at the cinema and we had religious school at the temple.

Our guru came from India to open the new temple. He arrived by helicopter on my school playing-field and then toured the area on an elephant in pouring rain. All the kids followed him for about five hours. Our guru is a religious teacher, he shows you how you can become a better person.

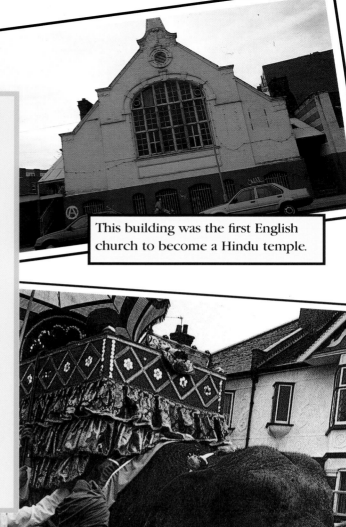

This building was the first English church to become a Hindu temple.

THE SAINT WHO WALKS AMONGST US

Interfaith Harmony ....

Close to God's creation ....

Lost in Meditation ....

blessing a cow

early morning worship

He loves equally, selflessly ....

Guru Pramukh Swami Maharaj with the Archbishop of Canterbury.

meeting the Archbishop of Canterbury, U.K.

comforting disabled children, Africa

Me in the front row at a wedding.

McDonalds opened in Wembley in the 1970s.

Like most Hindus we always ate vegetarian food at home, but my mum said I should eat meat when I was out if there wasn't any choice. I quite liked sausages and burgers so it was a great thing when McDonalds opened in Wembley. I stopped eating meat after I met our guru. He said I should become a vegetarian and that I shouldn't smoke or drink if I wanted to be a good Hindu.

We often went to family weddings at the weekends. There'd be a big party, it would go on a long time with lots of food and music. Some of my cousins had arranged marriages. Mostly, though, if a boy wanted to marry a girl he'd go to an older brother or uncle and say, "I want to marry so and so, please pass a message to her parents". If all the parents agreed, the wedding would go ahead. My mum might introduce me to a suitable girl when the time comes for me to marry and I certainly wouldn't marry anyone she didn't approve of.

I learnt a lot of Hindu stories from Indian comics.

Leaving school

Autumn .... Term, 19 79

Name... PATEL , Tarun .... Form... 4H ....

ALS

SUBJECT	YEAR FORM etc.	GRADE or %	EFFORT	
Religious Education	Form	C	C	Tarun m...
English Language	CSE	C	C	Tarun n... at home needs ca...
English Literature		C	C	Tarun ho... class w... please...
Mathematics	%C.S.E	C+	B	
Geography	E₁	D+	C+	Tarun to... but can... talkative... the pre...
Biology	4PH	D	C	Tarun work is always...
Physics	E₂	C	C	Tarun makes unsour... work
T.D.	4D2	C	D	Tarun but w... any...
Computer Studies	%/CSE	D	C	A disappo... spent less time talking in res... make far greater progress
P.E.	4HJ	C	B	Tarun has continued to prod...
Careers	H	-	B+	Satisfactory performance well in class.

A = EXCELLENT   B = VERY GOOD   C = AVERAGE

I was a very keen squash player at school. My coach was the British Airways champion and he encouraged me to become a pro. He even went as far as writing to my mother to say I should make a career of it. But what I really wanted to do was to get into business.

Economics really interested me but unfortunately I wasn't any good at the exams. After I got an unclassified in my CSE, the careers adviser said, "Don't even try for economics or accountancy, go for sociology or psychology". But I got an interview at Ealing College and begged for a place even though my grades were poor. I was lucky to get in.

I finished up with a BA Honours in economics. Now I work as a business adviser, finding money for new projects. I'd really like to go into hotel development here and in Europe, that's my ambition at the moment.

In the news

These are some of the important events which happened during Tarun's childhood.

1970 In Britain, eighteen-year-olds were able to vote for the first time. Labour lost the election and Edward Heath became Prime Minister.

1972 The miners' strike forced the government to introduce the three-day working week in order to save stocks of coal.

1973 Princess Anne married Captain Mark Phillips.

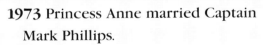

1973 Attacks on Israel by Egypt and Syria started the October War in the Middle East. Arab oil producers raised prices by 70% to put pressure on the USA to act against Israel.

1974 President Nixon resigned in Washington. Turkey invaded Cyprus and many Greek Cypriot refugees came to Britain.

1975 The American forces finally withdrew from South Vietnam.

1976 Concorde started passenger flights. Chairman Mao Tse-Tung, the Chinese leader, died.

1977 In 1977 there were street parties throughout Great Britain to celebrate the Queen's Silver Jubilee.

1978 The wrecked oil tanker *Amoco Cadiz* caused a pollution disaster in the English Channel.

1979 The Shah of Iran was overthrown and Ayatollah Khomeini returned from exile in Paris to take power.

Things to do

Make a 1970s scrapbook

Many of your relatives or neighbours will have memories of the 1970s. Their experiences may have been very different from those of Tarun Patel. Show them this book and ask them how their life in the 1970s compared.

If you have a cassette recorder you could tape their memories. Before you visit people, make a list of the things you want to talk about — for example, music, clothes, films, school, sports. Some people may have kept photos of the period as well as magazines or records. Ask if you can look at them.

Go to your local library. Ask to see any newspapers from the 1970s. Look at books about entertainment and fashion. Compare how things looked in the 1970s with how they look now. Your library may have a local studies section. If so, ask the librarian if they have any photographs of your area from the 1970s. Compare the houses and the shops then with what there is today. Walk around your area to see what shops and businesses might have started.

Look at adverts in old magazines, and compare the prices then with how much things cost now.

Use what you find out to make a scrapbook about the 1970s.

Reading list: here is a list of other books to read on the 1970s.

Decades: The Seventies
Michael Garrett (Wayland)

Finding out about life in Britain in the 1970s
Pamela Harper (Batsford)

Growing up in the 1970s
Nance Lui Fyson (Batsford)

History of the Modern World: The Seventies
John Edwards (Macdonald Educational)

Picture History of the Twentieth Century: 1970s
Tim Healey (Franklin Watts)

Portrait of a Decade: The 1970s
Elizabeth Campling (Batsford)

Index

Series design: David Bennett
Design: Mel Raymond
Editor: Jenny Wood

Picture research: Sarah Ridley
Printed in Belgium

Acknowledgements

The author and publisher would like to
thank Tarun Patel without whom this book
would not have been possible. Thanks also
to the Swaminarayan Temple, London.

Photography: Neil Thomson

Additional pictures: courtesy of Argos 23c;
courtesy of Capital Radio 18b; Design
Museum 19tl, 22c; Format/Raisa Page 16c,
17bl; John Frost Newspaper Service
endpapers; Greater London Record
Office/Grange Museum, London 10t, 14/15b;
Harrow and Wembley Observer Series 24br;
courtesy of McDonalds 25tr; National Film
Archive/Lucasfilms 19bc; National Film
Archive/Paramount 19tr; Newslink Africa
5c, 5b, 6c, 6b, 7c; Robert Opie 11br;
Popperfoto 6t, 17tl, 17tr, 27(all), 28(all),
29(all); courtesy of Raleigh Industries 23t;
Wembley History Society/Grange Museum,
London 8c, 13b 19br.

A CIP Catalogue record for this book
is available from the British Library.

Wednesday June 8 1977
No 60,024
Price fifteen pence

THE TIMES

Prince Charles on the Commonwealth's future: Special Report

One million people greet the Queen on her Silver Jubilee Day

By Penny Symon

The Queen drove in state through her capital to St Paul's yesterday to share in the Commonwealth's thanksgiving to God for her 25 years on the throne. The million people who cheered her on her way encompassed her with such an ocean of enthusiasm and affection as must have dispelled from her mind all consciousness of the cold and showers of her Silver Jubilee Day. Thousands had camped out all night to make sure of a glimpse of the Royal Family's glittering procession, and to add their quota to the deafening acclamations that accompanied them all the way.

After the service, the Queen's good humour was evident to all as she strolled with the Duke of Edinburgh from the cathedral to Guildhall for luncheon chatting with many in the crowd as she went. The formal and informal business of the day [reports and pictures, pages 2, 4 and 5] reached its conclusion, after the Royal Family's return to Buckingham Palace, when the Queen and her husband appeared on the balcony in reply to repeated cries from the crowd of "We want the Queen". They were rewarded with several appearances by the Queen and the Duke waving from the balcony.

Earlier, the processional route, via The Mall, Trafalgar Square, Strand, Temple Bar, Fleet Street, Ludgate Circus and Ludgate Hill, had been packed with people determined to show their affection for the Queen. They sang the National Anthem as she entered the cathedral, cheered her as she walked from there to Guildhall for luncheon, and on her return to the palace in an open landau.

The highlight of the day was the service at St Paul's, officially described as: "A form of prayer and thanksgiving to Almighty God commemorating the blessings granted to the Queen's most excellent Majesty during the 25 years of her reign."

It was one of those occasions that the British are still able to do so well. The pomp and pageantry were magnificent, everything ran like clockwork, and no one stumbled over his lines.

All those invited, except one, took their seats in plenty of time. The missing guest was Mr James Mancham, who was deposed as President of Seychelles soon after his arrival in London for the Commonwealth conference, which begins today.

The guest list, prepared by the Lord Chamberlain's Office, included Mr Mancham, but one of his aides, speaking from the Savoy Hotel, where Mr Mancham is staying, said he had decided not to attend the service because he was concerned about the attention he might attract. "It was the Queen's day, and he did not want his presence to detract from that."

The only other embarrassment, but one that the parties concerned carried off with great aplomb, was the fact that Lord Snowdon, who is separated from Princess Margaret, was seated eight rows behind the Royal Family. He watched his wife enter the cathedral in a procession with Lord Linley and Lady Sarah Armstrong-Jones, his children. When the service ended the children lefr the procession to greet their father affectionately in a side aisle.

After the main part of the congregation had been seated Commonwealth heads of state and leaders of delegations attending the Commonwealth conference took their seats in pews behind those reserved for the Royal Family. The Prime Minister helped to usher them to their seats, and had a quiet chat with several. Mrs Callaghan, in a straw hat adorned with bunches of red flowers, sat next to the King of Lesotho, who was wearing a bright military uniform decorated with much gold and blue.

The leaders included Archbishop Makarios, President of Cyprus, Dr Kenneth Kaunda, of Zambia, Dr Banda, of Malawi, Mr Trudeau, the Canadian Prime Minister, Sir Seretse Khama, President of Botswana, and Mr Lee Kuan Yew, Prime Minister of Singapore.

They, and the rest of the congregation of 2,700, were treated before the service began to the spectacle of several processions threading their way along to their allotted places.

They included archbishops and bishops, officers of the orders of chivalry, the Yeomen of the Guard, and the Honourable Corps of Gentlemen at Arms, resplendent in gold helmets decorated with white ostrich feathers, which were gently fanned by the light breeze in the cathedral.

Then the moment that all had been waiting for. People stood on tiptoe and craned their necks for a better view as members of the Royal Family began to arrive and settle into their places in the front pew, behind the red velvet chairs placed for the Queen and the Duke of Edinburgh.

As the royal ladies seated themselves the pew began to resemble a garden full of pastel-coloured flowers. All were dressed in varying shades of pink, lavender, blue, green and turquoise. Queen Elizabeth the Queen Mother's outfit was of a slightly darker shade of yellow than that of the Duchess of Gloucester, and Princess Margaret's pink was also a little darker than that of the Queen. The Duchess of Kent, who always manages to look a little different, was wearing a bright lettuce-green short-sleeved coat over a matching green and white dress.

The service began with the singing of the hymn "All people that on earth do dwell", the version arranged by Ralph Vaughan Williams for the Queen's coronation. The coronation of Edward VII and Queen Alexandra was recalled by the choir's singing of the anthem "I was glad".

The music for Psalm 121 was composed by Mr Barry Rose, sub-organist of St Paul's, and Mr Christopher Dearnley, the organist, composed the anthem based on Psalm 89.

The first lesson, from the Book of Micah, was read by the Archbishop of York, and the second, from St Matthew, by the Archdeacon of London, the Ven Sam Woodhouse.

The Archbishop of Canterbury, Dr Coggan, told the congregation that Britain and the Commonwealth had been blessed beyond measure by having at their heart an example of service untiringly done, of duty faithfully fulfilled, and of a home life stable and wonderfully happy.

"Many today are seeing through the hollowness of a way of life which seeks to build on a basis of materialism, of each for himself, or each for his sectional interest, and forgets the good of the whole", Dr Coggan said. "Many are seeing the supreme need for reconciliation and understanding at the heart of a people, where rivalry or suspicion could so easily lead to open conflict."

After the service the Queen spoke at a luncheon given by the Corporation of London at Guildhall. Eight hundred guests consumed salmon-trout, beef with potatoes, beans and carrots, and melon and raspberries, and then heard the Queen remark that in olden days jubilees were celebrated at the golden fiftieth year. There was a distinct sabbatical flavour about the proceedings, she said.

"It is beginning to dawn on me that a silver jubilee is of a somewhat different nature. But if this is not exactly a period of rest for us, it is certainly one of refreshment and of happiness and satisfaction."

The Queen's speech, page 4

All-night wait brings its own reward

By Roger Berthoud

Patience was rewarded for those who waited all night in Ludgate Hill and outside St Paul's, defying the adverse weather forecast and suffering the occasional shower, in order to enjoy a close look at the Queen.

Most of those in the front rows on the packed pavement before the cathedral had been there since midnight or earlier. "It was worth it", said Karen Budford, a trainee nursery nurse from Southend, Essex. "We got a superb view as she entered St Paul's and she will pass by us as she comes out."

She and others like her had no sleep and were soaked by a couple of heavy showers.

Part of the crowd joined in the singing as the strains of "Praise, my soul, the King of Heaven" wafted from St Paul's.

About ten minutes late, the Queen emerged from St Paul's and began her "walkabout" to Guildhall, accompanied by the Duke of Edinburgh, the Lord Mayor and the Lady Mayoress.

As she moved towards the garden on the north side of the cathedral Jennifer Williams, aged 13 from Tottenham, presented her with a bunch of roses and was asked whether she had picked them herself. The Duke asked Mrs Jill Finnegan, from Sydenham, whether her jubilee shopping bag contained today's supplies.

And so it went on, the royal couple pausing every 50 yards or so as they moved down Cheapside, whose pavements, lightly occupied earlier on, were now packed. "Greetings from Toowoomba, Queensland", proclaimed one banner.

David Summerhill, aged 8, gave her a drawing. "What did she say to you?", he was asked. "I forgot", he replied.

At the church of St Mary-le-Bow she stopped and was presented with a replica of Bow Bell by the rector, the Rev Joseph McCulloch, and signed a service book.

Martin Smith, a student from Middlesex Polytechnic, sought to vary the usual bland exchanges. "Is there a mechanical arm in your coat?", he asked, greatly daring. "I haven't reached that stage yet", our non-bionic Queen retorted.

As she turned into King Street, towards Guildhall, she paused again. "Are all these yours?", she asked Mrs Viveth Parkinson, from Jamaica, and Edmonton, London, pointing to the six smiling children in front of her. Only three were Mrs Parkinson's, the others being nephews and nieces.

Miraculously, the rain held off. After seeing the Queen safely into the new extension of Guildhall and watching her walk along the glass-sided ambulatory, past the pikemen to luncheon in the great hall, much of the crowd began to disperse and greatly warming was the crush in St Paul's Underground station thereafter.

A moment to be treasured for a lifetime as the Queen pauses to talk to some of the crowd lining the route during her walk from St Paul's Cathedral to Guildhall after yesterday's service of thanksgiving.

'Liz rules OK' the Cockney way

By Louis Heren

A large banner hung on the wall of the high-rise flats proclaimed: "Liz Rules. OK?", and far below in Havering Street they were celebrating her jubilee in the good old Cockney way.

A tea party and a fancy-dress competition for the kids, bottles of booze and dancing for the grown-ups and lashings of Cockney kindness and good humour for everybody. It was just as I remembered it when I grew up round the corner in High Street, Shadwell.

Mrs Anscombe at number 46 began raising money for the party last September, and with collections at the local bingo hall and elsewhere raised £621 for 20 street parties.

Mrs Jones, who lives at number 34 with her lorry-driver husband, and Mrs Frost down the street organized the kids' party. She said that she was a P & O stewardess, which translated means she is a char at the company's office in Leadenhall Street.

The bunting fluttered in the sun, and the kids tucked in while their dads reminisced. Nothing like a street party to keep people together, said a foreman who had to move down to Tilbury docks when they closed the London docks.

Not like the old days though, said a glass worker. The

Continued on page 4, col 1

President Amin 'arriving today in London' his Entebbe aide says

By Staff Reporters

President Amin of Uganda was said last night to be "on the high seas" and due to arrive in London this morning to attend the Commonwealth Conference.

A telephone call made by *The Times* to his command post in Entebbe extracted the information that the "Field Marshal and President for Life" had left yesterday morning to go to England "via Arab countries".

The voice at the end of the line also said that they were about to telephone Mr Callaghan to check on their President's exact whereabouts. But at midnight no message had been received in London.

Earlier, Uganda Radio announced that President Amin had arrived "at his first destination" though it did not say where this was. After making a stop in an Arab country, the radio went on, he is expected to sail to Britain either from France, West Germany or Ireland.

Throughout the day there were constant false alarms although no Ugandan flight appeared on British radar screens.

At 10 Downing Street a spokesman refused to say what preparations had been made to deal with President Amin's arrival. Nothing could be revealed because the policy was "to keep Amin off balance".

Then came reports that he may not have taken off at all because his bodyguard and advisers were still in Uganda. At lunchtime yesterday, the Irish government seemed to have put paid to this by announcing that a Ugandan aircraft was approaching Dublin.

No Ugandan aircraft materialized but the Belgian Government then announced that it would not allow any Ugandan aircraft to land. The Portuguese said they would permit a landing for emergency refuelling and the French promptly announced that they would allow a landing if permission were sought.

At the European air traffic control unit in Brussels there were no reports of any Ugandan aircraft flying nor of any flight plan filed. Nonetheless an unidentified transport aircraft with a fighter escort was seen over Calais and said to be heading for Britain.

A little later a Boeing 707 was sighted over Nice and reported to be heading f om Ethiopia towards Britain.

The Foreign Office could throw no light on what was going on. The Home Office said that immigration officials at airports and ports had been warned to be ready for President Amin.

Charles Harrison writes from Nairobi: Ugandans heard for the first time that President Amin had left for Britain in the mid-morning news broadcast from Kampala. The broadcast was delayed for 15 minutes, when it was announced that he had left on board an aircraft of a "friendly country" from an unnamed air base somewhere in Uganda soon after 3 am.

Late in the afternoon, the radio mentioned for the first time that he was heading for London to attend the Commonwealth Conference.

Christopher Walker writes from Dublin: The Irish coalition Government yesterday took time off from the serious business of electioneering to prepare itself and its country to repel an embarrassingly phantom invasion by President Amin.

By last night an atmosphere of farce had overtaken an exercise which began in deadly earnest earlier in the day with the dispatch of more than 50 armed troops, six Panhard armoured cars and an assortment of police dogs to Dublin airport.

The panic began shortly before lunch when a routine Irish Cabinet meeting was suddenly interrupted with the unwelcome news that the Ugandan President was heading for the Irish Republic en route to London. As faces later grew redder with his continuing non-arrival, official sources flatly refused to disclose the original source of the information but it is believed to have been an over-imaginative European diplomat based in Kampala.

Anxious to avoid a diplomatic incident, the Government quickly issued an official statement through its information service and every available press and television reporter was withdrawn from election coverage and hastily dispatched to the small airport.

Excitement increased to fever pitch during the afternoon when the control tower could distinctly be heard calling 10 times in succession: "Uganda flight 345. Do you read me?" This anxious message reaffirmed local conviction that Amin's plane was busily burning up fuel over the Irish Sea in order to demand emergency landing rights which the unwilling Irish authorities would be unable by international law to refuse.

But this false alarm, too, was eventually explained by a shamefaced official who summoned scores of correspondents and cameramen. It was a mistake, he explained, caused by airport controllers misreading the call sign of an Aer Lingus training flight in the vicinity.

Bomb alert on Mintoff plane

Ajaccio, June 7.—A British Airways Trident airliner carrying Mr Dom Mintoff, the Maltese Prime Minister, to the Commonwealth conference in London, today made an emergency landing here after a warning that there was a bomb on board. British Airways was expected to send another Trident to fly Mr Mintoff to London.—Reuter.

Dr Kaunda criticizes Britain, page 7; Words speak louder than action, page 14; Leading article, page 15.

Growth of Civil Service 'is under control'

Growth of the Civil Service has been brought under control, figures to be published on Friday are expected to show. Central government manpower remained steady at 746,000 in the six months until April 1 and is not expected to rise unless the Cabinet amends its system of cash limits. Combined with the general climate of restraint in Whitehall, the limits have been held responsible for the unexpectedly low manpower figures Page 6

£10m campaign for grocery shoppers

Grocery shoppers can expect price cuts or double stamp offers worth an estimated £10m during the next month as a result of the biggest sales battle since the trading stamp war of the early 1960s. The first campaign in this year's battle, set off by Tesco's decision to drop Green Shield stamps, started last night with a barrage of press and television advertisements Page 17

Ulster policeman shot

The comparative lull in violence in Belfast during the jubilee celebrations was shattered when a policeman was shot and severely wounded in Andersonstown and a restaurant in the north of the city was extensively damaged by a bomb and fire. The policeman was in a patrol car that came under fire from a house taken over by gunmen Page 6

Hostages set record

Proving more than a match for the Dutch authorities' strategy of patience, the South Moluccan gunmen holding 56 adult hostages took the siege into its sixteenth day, a record of its kind for Holland. The Dutch crisis cabinet again met in The Hague but is showing no signs of reopening the deadlocked attempts at mediation Page 6

50p school meals urged

Parents should have to pay the full economic cost of school meals, the National Association of Head Teachers, which represents two thirds of all head teachers in state primary schools decided at its conference in Southport. That would raise the cost from 15p to 50p Page 6

Threat to Zambia power

Mr Roger Hawkins, Rhodesian Minister of Combined Operations, threatened to cut off power supplies to Zambia from the Kariba hydroelectric complex if the Zambians did not stop unprovoked attacks on Rhodesian territory. In London for the Commonwealth conference, President Kaunda of Zambia said Britain was seriously mishandling its African policy Page 7

Abortion defeat: A surprise victory in the Italian Senate for opponents of the Abortion Bill could cause a serious upset in the country's delicate political balance 6

Lisbon: Portuguese Socialists reject coalition with any Opposition party 6

Seychelles: In the aftermath of the coup representation at the Commonwealth Conference remains uncertain Earlier story, 8

Turkey: Mr Ecevit solicits political support from dissidents and independents in forming a government 8

RECORD OF BORROWERS
IMPORTANT – Write your name in the
              space below.

NAME	CLASS	DATE TO BE RETURNED